SPORT &
ACTIVE LEISURE

Practical guides for practical people

In this increasingly sophisticated world the need for manually skilled people to build our homes, cut our hair, fix our boilers, and make our cars go is greater than ever. As things progress, so the level of training and competence required of our skilled manual workers increases. In this new series of career guides from Trotman, we look in detail at what it takes to train for, get into, and be successful at a wide spectrum of practical careers.

The *Real Life Guides* aim to inform and inspire young people and adults alike by providing comprehensive yet hard-hitting and often blunt information about what it takes to succeed in these careers.

Other titles in the series include:

THE ARMED FORCES

THE BEAUTY INDUSTRY

CARPENTRY & CABINET-MAKING

CATERING

CONSTRUCTION

ELECTRICIAN

ENGINEERING TECHNICIAN

HAIRDRESSING

INFORMATION & COMMUNICATIONS TECHNOLOGY

THE MOTOR INDUSTRY

PLUMBING

THE POLICE SERVICE

RETAILING

TRAVEL & TOURISM

WORKING OUTDOORS

WORKING WITH ANIMALS & WILDLIFE

WORKING WITH YOUNG PEOPLE

SPORT & ACTIVE LEISURE

ANGELA YOUNGMAN

Real Life Guide to Sport & Active Leisure

This first edition published in 2009 by Trotman Publishing,
an imprint of Crimson Publishing Ltd, Westminster House,
Kew Road, Richmond, Surrey TW9 2ND

© Trotman Publishing 2009

Author: Angela Youngman

Design by Nicki Averill

British Library Cataloguing in Publication Data
A catalogue record for this book is available from the British
Library

ISBN: 978-1-84455-198-9

Typeset by RefineCatch Ltd, Bungay, Suffolk

Printed and bound in Italy by LEGO SpA

CONTENTS

ABOUT THE AUTHOR

Angela Youngman is a qualified teacher working as a freelance journalist and author. She specialises in leisure, education, careers and gardening. Angela has written several books, including a series of 'How to' gardening books. As a journalist she has undertaken editorial work on a wide range of topics for numerous publications, as well as writing and compiling websites. She is married, has two children and lives in Norfolk.

FOREWORD

This *Real Life Guide to Sport & Active Leisure* offers practical information on every aspect of training for and finding a job in the field. Whether you are just starting out or looking for your next career move this book shows the different entry routes into the industry, gives you an outline of the jobs available, and explains the skills and attributes you need to be successful.

City & Guilds vocational qualifications support learners from pre-entry to professional level and we award over a million certificates every year. Our qualifications meet the latest industry requirements and are recognised by employers worldwide as proof that candidates have the knowledge and skills to get the job done.

We are delighted to be a part of the Trotman *Real Life Guides* series to help raise your awareness of these vocational qualifications – we are confident that they can help you to achieve excellence and quality in whichever field you choose. For more information about the courses City & Guilds offer check out www.city&guilds.com – get yourself qualified and see what you could do.

City & Guilds

INTRODUCTION

What comes into your mind when you think about careers in sport and active leisure? Highly paid footballers? Athletes spending long hours each day just perfecting their sport? Celebrity sportspeople taking part in TV game shows? Media coverage of high-profile sports events such as the Olympics, the Grand National and the FA Cup?

The next immediate thought is that 'careers in sport and leisure are not for me because my skills are not as good as those professional sportspeople'.

You could not be more wrong. You do not have to be a professional sportsperson to have a career in the sport and active leisure industry. Professional sportspeople make up a minority of the massive number of people who choose to participate in sports activities every day. This can range from swimming to weight training, horse riding to martial arts. To service this industry lots of people are needed. Around 2.5 million people work in the sport and active leisure sector – and these numbers are increasing every year. It is a growth sector with lots of opportunities for ambitious young people who are looking for interesting careers that can grow and develop in many different ways.

Millions of pounds are set to be invested in sport and active leisure over the next decade. The UK government has already indicated that it is putting money into schools, community sports, elite sports, coaching provision and training for PE teachers. It is also investing heavily in health and wellness programmes designed to decrease obesity and encourage people to get fit and live healthy lifestyles.

Don't forget too the fact that the UK is set to host several major international sports events over the next decade – the Olympics and Paralympics, the Commonwealth Games and the Women's Rugby World Cup. All of these events involve major investment and many new jobs. For example, in 2005 the International Olympic Committee indicated that the 2012 Olympics could lead to 70,000 new jobs and £17 billion investment.

There are opportunities to work overseas as well as within the UK. Working locations range from leisure centres to golf courses, hotels to shops, and offices to swimming pools. Think too of all the big sporting events attended by thousands of people, or watched by millions more on TV. People are needed to work behind the scenes, organising the day's activities, training the participants as well as providing media coverage. Without their help, such events could not take place.

Q DID YOU KNOW?

The 2004 Olympic Games in Athens was the most watched sporting event ever on television. Approximately 3.9 billion people worldwide tuned into the Games.

Self-employment within this booming sector is a definite option for keen and ambitious people. Successful businesses can be built up and created from very small beginnings.

Jobs covered in the sport and leisure sector fall into eight groups:

1. sports professionals
2. instructing and coaching
3 fitness training/sport and health
4. club and centre management
5. sport media, marketing and public relations (PR)
6. sponsorship, sports promotion and retailing
7. active leisure
8. practical work.

So is a career in sport and active leisure for you? If you have the right skills, interest and a flexible attitude to work, then the answer could well be yes. Very few people working in sport and leisure have a 9 to 5, Monday to Friday job. Many work weekends, evenings and on public holidays. Shift work is common. You have to be able to deal with all kinds of people, from children to adults, beginners to highly skilled sportspeople. You need to be able to think on your feet, to come up with solutions to problems quickly, and to deal with the unexpected. You need to be calm and not to panic. You can find out more about the skills required to work in sport and leisure in Chapter 5, Tools of the Trade.

DID YOU KNOW?

One billion people, or 15% of the world's population watched the opening ceremony of the Beijing Olympics.

If you are likely to be seeking self-employment or eventually aiming to set up a small business, basic business skills are essential. This includes an ability to work on your own, to accept responsibility for your own future, to set your own budgets and deal with finances, as well as marketing your activities.

To find out more about potential career opportunities, browse through the pages of this book. It will highlight the type of careers that can be found, including details of training and future prospects. There are case studies of people working in the sector, talking about their jobs and how they have developed interesting careers. There is also a fun quiz to see how much you really know about sport and active leisure!

Also included are sections on how to find out whether you have the right personal qualities to make a successful career in sport and active leisure, as well as lots of contact addresses and websites of professional organisations and training providers for you to find out more.

CHAPTER 1
SUCCESS STORY

STUART PERRY
Golf professional

26-year-old Stuart Perry has the job of his dreams – teaching golf aboard a cruise ship. He is a PGA Professional with Elite Golf Cruises and explains how it has all come about.

'I played golf from a very early age and when I was 16 years old I knew I wanted to go professional. I had played at county level but was interested in the teaching side as I knew I was not good enough to be competitively professional. I joined the 3-year PGA course and worked at Telford Golf and Country Club while I trained.'

He worked there until 2004, before moving to Premier Golf Products Limited and then to Swingers Golf Centre. Then in 2007, everything changed.

'I was thinking about working abroad but didn't see anything that would be any different to working in the UK. A friend, Simon, was working as a director of golf at a Breezes Golf Club so I contacted him to see if he had a job. There wasn't anything at the time, but he said he'd let me know if anything came up. A few weeks later he had a golf tour from a cruise ship at the club. He got talking to one of the fleet trainers, who told him of an opening, and Simon gave him my number.

'I spoke to them on the Monday, packed my suitcase, flew to Denmark on the Thursday and that was it.'

Since then he has been working for Elite Golf Cruises, touring the world aboard a luxury liner, *Carnival Pride*, teaching golf to passengers and seeing the world – a long way from his initial start working in a pro shop and teaching on the driving range. Instead he has played golf with numerous celebrities, including pop star Robbie Williams, and travels all round the world.

'You are away from England for 6–8 months at a time. Because of potential problems out at sea, like a fire or if we have to abandon ship, everyone is responsible for the safety of the passengers. You have to be ready for any eventuality at any time, so you can never be drunk or you'll be sent straight home – that's probably the worst rule.

Everything has to be done to a strict timetable. If you miss the ship, you have to meet it at the next port. Everything has to go to plan or it could cost the cruise company millions of dollars.

The one thing I prefer most working here rather than England, though, is the weather. The ships always travel to where the weather's best and everyone is on holiday, so they're in great spirits.

We get all sorts of people who come onto the ship and want to play golf. I try to push for beginners to give the sport a go while they are on holiday. I have also had club pros on board and celebrities.

I get my own cabin and have my food and accommodation paid for. I have no bills to pay, it's tax-free earnings and I work on commission, so I get out of it what I put in.

I have guidelines on hours I have to work, but I teach or play golf at every opportunity I have.'

As the only pro on board the ship Stuart is kept busy, taking lessons from 9 a.m. until 8 p.m. When the ship docks, he can take from four to 40 golfers ashore to play one of the courses. Apart from working as a golf pro, Stuart is also expected to undertake safety checks and perform specific tasks in the event of an emergency.

He says:

'My days do vary. The first day of the cruise is embarkation. This is where I work at the excursion desk, taking bookings and speaking to the passengers about the golf programme.

Once we're under way I take lessons. The ship has a practice net at the back, which is cool, as I have awesome views and get to work on my tan while teaching. We also have a putt putt course on the ship.'

In the old days, passengers used to be able to smash balls off the ship and into the ocean. They even had balls made of fish food. Those days are gone now, due to environmental guidelines.'

Stuart is pushing to be the number one pro within Elite Golf Cruises. He explains:

'The fleet has a leader board of all the pros, and we are regularly compared to the other pros in the Carnival fleet. There are 21 ships in the fleet and I'm in the top five each week. It's nice to be at the top.'

Not only does he get to spend all day every day with stunning ocean views, there are also stopoffs at courses worldwide.

'My favourite course is White Witch in Montego Bay, Jamaica. It's built in the rainforest with ocean views on most holes – it's breathtaking. Also the Desert Course at Cabo Del Sol in Mexico is amazing. It's like playing golf in Arizona, but with ocean views.

I get to see parts of the world I never thought I would. I get to wake up in a different country each day and play some of the best and most beautiful courses in the world. Each cruise I meet lots of new people. I work with other crew members from over 50 countries and I have friends in almost every country imaginable.'

CHAPTER 2
WHAT'S THE STORY?

Sport and active leisure is an industry which is wider and offers more varied career opportunities than you might expect. Even when there is not much money around, the sport sector continues to do well. It has been suggested that with people spending fewer hours at work they will be even more involved in sport and active leisure. Everyone is being encouraged to live active, healthy lives.

It is not just children and young people who are involved. Older people and retired people are active participants, trying new and unusual sports including bungee jumping and off-piste skiing.

SO WHAT IS SPORT AND ACTIVE LEISURE?

It covers everything from traditional sports played by competitive and often professional sportspeople to ways of encouraging ordinary people to get some exercise. This can range from visiting gyms to running marathons, from dancing to horse riding, attending playschemes to taking part in motor sports such as drag car racing. People are needed to teach and organise all these events, as well as run the organisations which deal with them. Physical activity which involves socialising at the same time tends to be the most popular. The range of sporting leisure activities outside the home is infinite; there are, for example, dozens of minor sports that can attract large audiences as well as high numbers of participants.

Sport and active leisure is a growth sector and there are no signs of this changing. Overall, one in four of all new jobs are to be found within sport and active leisure, with around 2.5 million people working in the sector. The total amount of money people spend on sport is estimated to be around £11.5 billion nationwide per year. This covers everything from the costs of participating to equipment, clothing, footwear and admissions to live sporting events. The government, Sports England and other organisations are seeking to increase the rate of sport participation among the population as part of the legacy of the 2012 Olympics. Several billion pounds are spent each year by local authorities, sports councils and the government so as to ensure that the majority of people have access to sports and active recreational facilities.

SPORT FOR LEISURE

Football remains the most popular sport. According to market research surveys 11.6% of adults play football either regularly or occasionally. Despite this, the most noticeable trend in recent years has been a move away from traditional sports to 'fitness' activities such as working out in gyms, visiting swimming pools, jogging and cycling. The majority of people participating in sport and active leisure are not involved in competitive sports. It is estimated that around 12% of the UK population visits a health and fitness club or leisure centre regularly, while many more visit on an occasional basis or take part in non-competitive sports. Even in a recession, people continue to participate in sporting activities because they enjoy them, and because they want to remain healthy. The only difference can be that people may opt for less expensive options.

HEALTH CLUBS AND LEISURE CENTRES

The UK health clubs and leisure centres market is split into two sectors: health clubs (privately owned businesses) and leisure centres (usually owned by local authorities). There are new health clubs, spas and leisure facilities opening throughout the country. It is a successful industry. By the end of March 2007, there were 5,714 fitness sites across the UK plus 3,117 private clubs and 2,597 gyms within sports centres. Gyms, fitness and leisure centres are always busy, and thousands of people each year take part in various outdoor pursuits.

INTERNATIONAL SPORTS IN BRITAIN

Sport and leisure looks set to become even more popular over the next few years, with a series of international sporting events being held in the UK. In 2009, Britain is set to host nine key sporting events, including the ICC World Cricket Twenty20 tournament, the World Modern Pentathlon Championships and the Artistic Gymnastics World Championships. During 2010/11 there will be the Women's Rugby World Cup, the European Water Ski Championships and the Badminton World Championships.

The biggest event comes in 2012, when the Olympics and Paralympics are held in London. In 2014 Glasgow will be hosting the Commonwealth Games. The UK is also hoping to host the 2013 Rugby Union World Cup, the 2015 Rugby League World Cup and the 2018 Football World Cup.

Already a massive publicity campaign focusing on the Olympics has begun, seeking to encourage more and more people to get involved in sports activities. The arrival of the

DID YOU KNOW?

The Olympic Flag was first flown in 1920 at the Antwerp Olympics. It is purposely designed to link together every country in the world. The five rings represent the continents: Americas, Europe, Asia, Africa and Australasia. The colours too are carefully chosen. Each nation in the world has at least one of the five colours – blue, yellow, black, green and red – in their national flag.

Olympics means thousands more jobs will become available within the Olympics organisation as well as within sports governing bodies and local authorities. This will not be limited to London – job opportunities will be created nationwide. The aim is to make the Olympics a signal to create a new generation of potential medal winners. This will have a knock-on effect throughout the country, ensuring the improvement of facilities and levels of tuition.

Many new centres are being built. In Suffolk, for example, work is under way on the world's first indoor winter sports resort. Built in a disused quarry, it will contain Europe's largest indoor ski slope, the UK's first Centre of Excellence for winter sport and act as a site for 14 winter sports in one location. It includes a new full-size ice rink, the first built for decades.

HEALTH AND FITNESS

The growth of the sport and active leisure sector is also helped by the fact that the government wants to improve people's health by encouraging them to get involved in sport. More and more people are obese – that is, extremely overweight – and it is not just adults. There has been a dramatic increase in childhood obesity: 16.9% of boys and 16.8% of girls aged 2 to 10 years in England are currently classified as obese, an increase from 9.6% and 10.3% respectively in 1995.

As a result, the government is investing money in sport and active leisure, including school sports and community facilities. As part of this investment, Sport England has recently launched a £36 million 'Sport Unlimited' project, which will make a major contribution to the government's target of giving children and young people the opportunity to do five hours of PE and sport a week at school and in the community. The scheme is being rolled out nationwide and will allow 900,000 more 11- to 19-year-olds to choose from a vast range of sports, including sailing, cycling, dodgeball, snowboarding, skiing and American football. Under the scheme, young people are offered 10-week taster sessions in

GOLDEN OLDIES

Margaret Wilcox Richards (1893–1999) took part in the Golden Age Games, winning gold medals for canoeing from age 91 until she was 103. She only stopped because she couldn't see properly.

Adeline Ablitt took up swimming when she was in her nineties and learned to fly a glider when she was 95. She even looped the loop!

sports which they have requested. The aim is to get at least 300,000 participants to join clubs and continue with sports when the 10 weeks are up.

Doctors frequently send patients to gyms to get fit. Leisure centres and gyms are focusing on activities designed to appeal to people wanting to get fit, families and older people. There are also work-related initiatives such as Active at Work in which businesses encourage employees to join health and fitness clubs or take part in sports-related activities. All this means even more job opportunities for people keen on developing a career in sport and active leisure.

OPPORTUNITIES WORLDWIDE?

Worldwide, there has been an increase in interest in sport and active leisure. International hotels and cruise ships require staff to supervise and instruct. Active holidays involving trekking, canoeing and white water rafting need instructors and leaders. New centres for active leisure are constantly opening. Adventure holiday company PGL, for example, opened five new centres in 2009, adding to its total of 38 centres across the UK, France and Spain.

Many health clubs operate in more than one country. Fitness First is the largest health club operator in the UK and Europe, with

150 clubs in the UK, 128 in Europe, plus 25 in East Asia and 39 in Australia. To take another example, Living Well is part of the international Hilton Group plc. It has 50 clubs throughout the UK and Ireland employing around 2,000 people and an overseas network in Australia, Germany, Turkey, Malta and Brazil. Virgin Active has 72 clubs in the UK and 167 worldwide – and is already planning to open 30 more clubs in Europe over the next few years.

NEW SPORTS AND ACTIVITIES

Further job opportunities are arising from the fact that new job categories are constantly emerging. Personal trainers were unknown a decade ago; now they are to be found in health clubs, gyms and leisure centres throughout the country. Many personal trainers are self-employed and have a good income. Parakiting – using kites to power yourself along the sand on buggies or skateboards – is a sport that has only become popular over the past few years. Now it is found worldwide, with UK experts spending time overseas providing tuition.

There are roller-skating centres in almost every town. Sports such as BMX biking, roller blading and snowboarding began

---

EXTREME IRONING

One of the strangest new sports is extreme ironing. Amazing but true! Participants aim to find the weirdest and most dangerous place in which to do some ironing – underwater, in a shark tank, surfing, BMX biking, snorkelling, up a mountain, or even while jumping off a cliff wearing a parachute. A 4-man team won the World Extreme Ironing Championships by climbing 5,500 feet up a mountain in the French Alps in order to do their sport. Devised by rock climber Phil Shaw, the sport has been taken up enthusiastically across Europe, particularly in Germany.

---

as teenage rebellion against organised sports. They have now become international, with world championships and professional players. Ice dancing and ice skating is steadily growing in popularity, fuelled partly by television programmes and touring ice shows. This in turn is creating a demand for teachers and new facilities.

A big growth area is paintballing. Over the past decade, numerous paintball sites have been created nationwide. Participants take part in a themed scenario organised by a marshal. They may have to capture an opposing group's headquarters, steal a flag or rescue someone from terrorists. If shot with a paintball, a participant is 'dead' for the remainder of that particular scenario. The game has widespread appeal, from children and teenagers to adults. Often businesses use paintballing sessions to develop teamwork skills among their employees. Imaginative companies such as Skirmish even run birthday party sessions.

Some paintball companies also offer lasertag activities. Just as with paintballing, lasertag can be played outside in the woods or inside at specialist centres. Each game has a set storyline – chase a sniper, capture a fort or flag. Participants have to wear helmets containing special probes. These are linked by wire to the participant's laser gun. Lives are lost whenever a laser bolt hits a probe. The advantage of this game is that it encourages longer participation, since each player has 10 lives and can often restore lives by returning to a set point during a game.

Active play is another activity which is growing rapidly. This involves working with children in playschemes, after-school and holiday clubs encouraging them to take part in sports and use playgrounds. It now accounts for 23% of the active leisure sector, with a total of 132,730 people employed across the UK. The sector has a £1.5 billion turnover.

DID YOU KNOW?

Olympic woman weightlifter Cheryl Haworth can lift the equivalent of two fridges over her head.

The government has specified that active play is of major concern, since it is a way of encouraging healthy living, as well as ensuring children have opportunities to fulfil their potential. It has awarded thousands of pounds to local councils to develop active play in their areas. More and more local councils are hiring play specialists capable of running children's holiday activity programmes. Play rangers work part-time with children, supervising after-school activities or playgrounds, encouraging them to play all manner of games from football to tag, as well as using the equipment on site.

OUTDOOR ADVENTURE

Another new activity which has emerged over the past decade is forest adventures. One of the most well-known companies in this field is Go Ape, which has attracted over 1,000,000 adventure seekers climbing rope ladders up into the trees, experiencing the thrills of trekking from tree to tree some 40 ft above the forest floor. Go Ape was established in 2002 by husband and wife team Tristram and Rebecca Mayhew. They discovered the concept while visiting the Auvergne National Forest in France. They watched a family swinging through the tree canopy, and noticed that adults and children alike were having a fantastic time. It convinced them that there was an opportunity to introduce similar centres in the UK.

There are now 17 centres across the UK, and there are plans to open 40 courses by 2012. Around 15 jobs are created on each site. Typical jobs include high ropes instructors and management positions. According to Tristram Mayhew, 'creating adventures and encouraging others to live life more adventurously is the ethos behind Go Ape. It's very much about introducing people, young and old, to the forest and being able to explore the forest from a different perspective.' Forests have become locations for a range of sports and fitness activities including husky racing, orienteering and tree canopy walking.

As part of the move towards reclamation and improving the environment, it is now a condition of quarrying and mining that, after materials have been extracted, the area has to be landscaped. For many quarries and rivers with historic industrial use, this means they have been turned into safe places for water sports and fishing. For example, even a small quarry can be quickly transformed into an area with organised sailing, swimming, canoeing and other water activities. Every time this happens, there is a need for people to manage the site, teach and supervise the public activities.

SPONSORSHIP, MARKETING AND RETAIL

Other booming areas of the sport and leisure industry are activities such as sports sponsorship, sports marketing and sports retail. Hosting major events is expensive, so sponsorship from businesses and other organisations is frequently sought using the aid of specialist companies. Sponsorship is currently valued at £350 million and deals can vary from £50 to £500 million depending on the opportunity. High-profile agreements include squad sponsorship such as Norwich Union and the GB Athletics team; Speedo and Mark Foster; Heineken and ITV's Rugby World Cup coverage.

DID YOU KNOW?

Wearing Adidas shoes, Emil Zatopek won three gold medals in one week at the 1952 Olympic Games – the 5,000 metres, 10,000 metres and the marathon. This has never been repeated, either in or out of Adidas shoes.

Likewise marketing events is important so that maximum numbers of people come to see them or watch the events on TV.

Another popular sector is sports retail. Every high street and out-of-town shopping area has at least one sports retailing store, sometimes more.

WHAT CAN SPORT AND LEISURE OFFER TO YOU?

It offers a varied and challenging career with lots of opportunities. It is a business area which includes lots of sports and activities that 20 years ago were either unknown, not invented or the preserve of a few enthusiasts. The internet means that something developed in one country, rather than taking decades to spread, can be well known worldwide within months. So for anyone in the industry, learning new skills and sports and ideas is essential for a long and interesting career. Equipment, laws and ideas on health and fitness all change at a rapid pace so it is vital to keep up with what is happening.

Any sport or activity, whether it is old or very new, can go in and out of fashion. Torvill and Dean's Olympic victories made ice skating very popular. Thousands of people took it up, competitions boomed and new rinks were built. By 2006, ice skating in the UK was declining, with few skaters reaching international competitions and the handful of remaining ice rinks struggling for survival. *Dancing on Ice* revitalised the sport and there are now more people than ever taking it up, and new ice rinks appearing. Not all sports are as lucky; for some the decline is permanent. This makes it doubly important for anyone considering a specialist role to plan ahead and remain flexible.

The sport and active leisure industry is characterised by a young workforce. According to the SkillsActive Skills Needs Assessment for England 2005, the sport and leisure industry has a higher proportion of young people aged 16 to 24 years old working in it than the national workforce overall. In total the sport and active leisure sector employs over 634,000 people in England alone – and around 18% of employers are reporting skill gaps among the workforce.

Starting salaries are generally from £10,000 upwards depending on the job, skills and experience you already possess. Someone who has relevant sports qualifications, first aid certificates or experience with children and young people may well start at a higher rate.

Full-time careers are not always possible within many areas of sport and leisure. Instead people may have to combine several activities in order to make a full-time job. An activity instructor might teach several subjects, or a coach might also work as a sports administrator. Flexibility and versatility are essential. Although the range of jobs is very wide, one common theme is that it is not for those who want Monday to Friday, 9 to 5 desk work.

Career development within sport and active leisure is rarely straightforward and may mean moving around the country, as Paul Esson from Kingswood – a company which runs adventure holidays for schools at sites throughout the UK – explains:

'I started as a kitchen assistant on the island in September 2003 as there were no instructor vacancies at the time. I went to instructor training at Overstrand in Norfolk, in January 2004. I got off to a good start by winning "Instructor of the Month" and was made Senior Group Leader for Camp Beaumont in July. In September 2004 I was promoted to Activity Senior Instructor, which involved transferring to Staffordshire.

I stayed as a senior instructor until March 2005, when I was promoted to Activity Co-ordinator and spent the rest of 2005 in Staffordshire. I was Assistant Camp Director for Camp Beaumont in 2005. In January 2006 I was transferred to Peak Venture as Activity Co-ordinator and stayed there until June, when I moved across to West Runton to be Assistant Camp Director again for Camp Beaumont.'

QUIZ

If you've read through the last few pages, you should have quite a good idea of whether you're interested in a career in sport and active leisure. If you think you are, why not test your knowledge and suitability a little further by completing the following short quiz. For each question, just choose which option you think is correct or the closest to what you think your response would be, and compare it with the answers at the end of the chapter. Don't worry if you get any questions wrong; it's only meant to be a bit of fun.

1 **Everyone knows where the Olympics began, but where did the Paralympics begin?**
A. Greece.
B. UK.
C. USA.

2 **Where is Europe's longest indoor ski slope going to be constructed?**
A. France.
B. Sweden.
C. England.

3 **What is the world's oldest continuous sporting event?**
A. Doggett's Coat and Badge Race (Rowing).
B. St Leger Horse Race.
C. English Football League Championship.

4 **Why do men and women no longer compete together in Olympic sharp shooting?**
A. Because the women shot too many men.
B. Because men were better than women.
C. Because women were better than the men.

5 **Why is a marathon called a marathon?**
A. After a chocolate bar.
B. After an Ancient Greek battle.
C. After a car.

6 **How many marathons are held each year?**
A. 800+
B. 700+
C. 600+

7 **What are the Ashes?**
A. Burnt pieces of wood.
B. Burnt pieces of ball.
C. Burnt pieces of coal.

8 **Which is the oldest cycling tour?**
A. Tour de Giro.
B. Tour de Vuelta.
C. Tour de France.

9 **Who is the most successful Formula One driver?**
A. Michael Schumacher.
B. Alain Prost.
C. Ayrton Senna.

10 **Badminton was invented by**
A. Riders at Badminton, when bad weather stopped the event.
B. British soldiers in India.
C. Sir Henry Badminton.

11 **Table tennis was originally called**
A. Tennis at the table.
B. Whiff Whaff.
C. Ping Pong.

12 **One of the world's best known sports clothing brands is:**
A. Nikon.
B. Nicki.
C. Nike.

ANSWERS

1. B. The Paralympics began in England at Stoke Mandeville Hospital
    in 1948 as a competition for wheelchair athletes. It quickly gained
    international renown, and disabled athletes from many countries took
    part. The games now take place just after the Summer Olympics and
    in the same location. Activities on offer include pentathlon, fencing,
    swimming, archery, snooker. There are also winter games, which
    include Nordic skiing.

2. C. SnOasis, the new winter sports centre being built in Suffolk, will
    house the largest indoor ski slope in Europe. It will be 415 metres
    long with a 70-metre vertical drop. The ski slope will be capable of
    being used for international competitions. It will have a capacity for
    2,400 skiers per hour. The centre will also have a 400-metre speed
    skating track, a 16-metre ice climbing wall, a full size ice rink, a
    1.5-kilometre cross country ski run and a 100-metre dry bobsleigh
    run. It will act as a UK centre for training young winter sports athletes.
    Overall it is the world's first indoor winter sports resort.

3. A. Doggett's Coat and Badge Race is the world's oldest continuous
    sporting race. The contest has been held on the River Thames every
    year since 1715. The St Leger race began in 1776, and the English
    Football League Championship did not start until 1877.

4. C. Sharpshooter Zhang Shan beat 40 men and five women in the
    1992 Olympics to gain a gold medal. After that men and women no
    longer competed together.

5. B. In Ancient Greece, the Athenians and Persians were at war. A
    decisive battle was fought at Marathon on the coast of Greece.
    Legend states that a runner called Pheidippides ran without stopping
    to Athens to announce that the Persians had been defeated in the

Battle of Marathon. He announced his news, collapsed and died. When the first Modern Olympics was set up, it was decided to hold a major race which recalled the glory of the Ancient Greeks. Since then marathons have been held at every Olympics and have been created as long-distance road races all over the world. In 1921, the length of a marathon was fixed at 42.195 km (26.22 miles). This length reflects the approximate distance between Marathon and Athens.

6. A. Over 800 marathons are held worldwide every year, with more than 82 countries involved and attended by thousands of runners. The biggest are held in Boston, New York City, Chicago, London and Berlin. The most unusual include marathons on the Great Wall of China and an intercontinental one which involves running across Europe and Asia. There is even a Polar Circle marathon, which is held on the Greenland ice cap in temperatures of $-15°C$.

7. B. The Ashes is the most famous trophy in cricket. It is given each year for test matches between England and Australia. The prize came about as a result of a joke. In 1882, England lost to Australia and the *Sporting Times* joked that English cricket was dead and should be burned, with the ashes being taken to Australia. The following year, when the English team visited Australia, it was given a tiny urn containing the burnt bails from a wicket used in the third test. Since then, whichever team wins the England–Australia test series is said to have won the Ashes. However, the Ashes do not move from country to country. The urn is kept permanently at Lord's Cricket Ground, London.

8. C. The Tour de France is not only the world's oldest but is also the most well-known cycling tour. It was first staged in 1903, when riders were expected to cycle a distance of 2,428 kilometres in six stages. The course has steadily grown and now contestants face a gruelling race of over 5,000 kilometres across a variety of terrain. They have to complete the course in 20 stages. A yellow jersey (the 'maillot jaune') is always worn by the current overall time leader. Around 15 million people watch the race, lining the streets to see the cyclists pass by. The Vuelta is a cycling Tour of Spain, and the Giro is a Tour of Italy.

9. A. Michael Schumacher is the world's most successful Formula One driver. He has won seven world titles (1994, 1995, 2000, 2001, 2002, 2003, 2004) and has also gained a record for the most race wins

within a season. In 2004 he had 13 race wins, giving him an overall total of 83, compared with Alain Prost's 51 and Ayrton Senna's 41.

10. B. Badminton was invented by British soldiers in Pune, India in the 19th century. As the city of Pune was formerly known as Poona, the game was also called Poona. When the officers returned to England, they brought the game with them. In 1873, it was renamed badminton following a garden party at Badminton House, the home of the Duke of Beaufort. Official rules had been created by 1877 and a governing body set up in 1893.

11. B and C. The game has its origins in England as an after-dinner amusement for upper-class Victorians in the 1880s. Mimicking the game of tennis in an indoor environment, everyday objects were originally enlisted to act as the equipment. A line of books would be the net, a rounded top of a champagne cork or knot of string as the ball, and a cigar box as the racket. Early rackets were often pieces of parchment stretched upon a frame, and the sound made gave the game its first nicknames of 'whiff whaff' and 'ping pong'.

12. C. Nike Inc produces footwear, clothing, equipment and accessory products for the sports and athletic market. It is the largest seller of such garments in the world. It sells to 140 countries around the world. Nike was founded in 1968 by Phil Knight.

CHAPTER 3
WHAT ARE THE JOBS?

When thinking about careers in sport and leisure, most people immediately think of athletes, footballers and other competitors playing games at very high standards. This can be off-putting for people who enjoy sports but do not have the desire or skill to play professionally.

The good news is that no matter what your level of sports skill, if you want a career in this sector then there are lots of opportunities. In fact, the job possibilities are far wider than you might expect. Sport and active leisure covers much more than just the well-known activities such as athletics, football and cricket. There are a wide range of minority sports which are attracting ever-increasing attention from keen sports enthusiasts as well as people who just want a new interest. Such activities include canoeing, dragon-boat racing, ice skating, parakiting, mountaineering, caving, martial arts, golf, sailing, motor sports, and cycling. Then there are the ever-increasing numbers of leisure centres, spas and private gyms, all of which need staff; likewise activity schemes, play work and holiday organisations.

If you are considering self-employment or have a desire to run your own business, the sport and active leisure sector offers considerable potential. Travel is also possible — acquiring skills as an instructor or play leader, for example, could result in working all over the UK and overseas. There is lots of demand for well-trained people to operate sports centres and teach minority sports worldwide. Even cruise ships have a large sports personnel

NEW EXTREME SPORTS

Sportspeople are always coming up with new ideas to expand their skills. New Zealand is one of the most creative in this respect. Having already given us the sports of bungee jumping and zorbing (going downhill in a plastic sphere), what is likely to come next? New Zealanders are currently enjoying the delights of:

▶ Fly by Wire: the fastest tethered adventure flight in the world. You are strapped in a part-plane, part-rocket machine as it hurtles around in a circle, tethered to a steel cable at speeds of up to 106 miles per hour. As it accelerates you experience a force of 3Gs to weightlessness within a 3-second interval. The flight lasts 6 minutes.

▶ Black Water Rafting (also called cave tubing). This involves floating through a pitch-black cave with a big rubber inner tube fitted around your waist or bottom – having first jumped 2 metres off a ledge into the inky blackness of the cave.

▶ Liquid-zorbing. Two or three buckets of water are added to the zorb, and you remain unattached to the inner ball while tumbling like a roller-coaster down a hill.

▶ Hydro-zorbing across the surface of a lake. You are left to flail about in the zorb as it floats across the water.

contingent. Swimming pools need attendants and lifeguards, while golf and other sports are frequently played on board ship with tuition being made available from skilled personnel.

Remember, too, that you do not have to be able-bodied in order to have a career in sports. There has been a massive growth in disabled sports and numerous opportunities are appearing for disabled people to become involved in areas such as coaching or working in the administration of leisure centres, gyms, ice rinks and roller-skating rinks.

When considering a career in sport and leisure, bear in mind that almost all jobs in this sector will require you to get out and about working in a variety of locations, often outside. You will not be confined to an office. Bear in mind, too, that you will not spend all of your time playing games and sports at the level to which you are accustomed. There will be lots of other activities that have to be done, such as administration, and the majority of teaching is undertaken at a fairly basic level.

So what types of jobs are available? Almost every single sport requires instructors and a few examples are given here. Then there are management opportunities, lifeguards, coordinators, centre operators. The choice is vast and the career potential equally wide. Once in the sector, career development can go in many different directions. The choice is up to you.

SPORTS PROFESSIONALS

The majority of sports professionals are people who have been playing their sport and competing from a very early age. They have reached a high standard and may compete as amateurs or professionals in a wide range of sports including athletics, cycling, equestrian sports, golf, motor sport, football and tennis. Opportunities also exist for people to become professional jockeys, as, unlike other sports, training for jockeys generally begins around age 16 years or over.

Most professional sports have people who act as judges for competitions and matches. Most of these are amateur, or are paid a small fee. There are a few sports where, at the highest level of the game, judges are full-time professionals. The main route into this is as an ex-sports professional, but the modern

DID YOU KNOW?

In 1991 Anthea Farrell became the first female jockey to win at Aintree when she won the John Hughes Memorial Trophy on J J Henry.

pace of some games means that more people are encouraged to enter it. It is almost impossible to go straight into these top levels; you have to work your way up through lower levels of the sport, often on a part-time or unpaid basis. The handful of professional judges include football referees, cricket umpires, ice-hockey and boxing referees.

INSTRUCTING AND COACHING

This is a constantly expanding area and one which offers lots of opportunities for career development. Instructors and coaches work with people at every level of sport to teach and improve skills. Instructors are needed for every sport that is practised within the UK, such as athletics, gym, riding, Pilates, hill walking, skating, swimming. Most instructors are qualified to teach several sports, as this offers the widest job opportunities. Coaches are slightly more specialised in that they tend to focus much more upon professional sportspeople, working mainly on a one-to-one basis to find ways of improving performance. Overall, there are more employment possibilities for instructors than there are for coaches.

Working locations vary according to the sport involved – it may be in gyms, outside on athletics tracks, football fields or amongst trees as a high-wire specialist or in riding stables. Hours tend to be long and irregular, and may be seasonal. Most instructors have to teach several sports and be constantly willing to learn new ones and gain appropriate qualifications in order to make a living on a full-time basis.

Salaries range from £10,000 upwards, with freelancers earning anything from £10 to £30 an hour. Career development can involve moving into leadership and management roles, human resources, sports development, marketing and facilities management. Some sectors, such as Pilates and horse riding, often provide an opportunity for self-employment or the setting up of a new business.

FITNESS TRAINING/SPORTS AND HEALTH

Given the ever-increasing prominence being placed on healthy lifestyles and using sport as a means to get fit, it is not surprising that demand for people who specialise in this area is constantly growing. Personal trainers began appearing 10 years ago, initially very much as a fad among young urban professionals. Now they have moved into mainstream sports activity with their services being taken up by a wide range of people. Communication skills – especially tact and patience – are essential, since the work involves getting unfit people fit by devising programmes and encouraging people to maintain their efforts until the required levels of fitness are reached.

On-the-job training is common among fitness instructors. Further training can allow you to become an advanced instructor, or to specialise in areas such as physical activity programmes to deal with obesity, back pain or coronary heart disease. Although many fitness instructors are employed by organisations, there are large numbers of self-employed instructors who rent space in a gym or set up their own facilities. Income can vary considerably. Freelance instructors earn around £20 to £40 an hour, while full-time trainers can earn up to £40,000 a year.

STRANGE SPORT

One of the most unusual sports possible takes place every year in Finland – and is certainly the place to go if you do not like mobile phones! The world championship in mobile phone throwing has been held every year since 2000. Contestants can take part in team or individual events. The phones get thrown some distance, too. In 2002, one contestant threw a Nokia 5110 phone a total distance of 66.72 metres.

Many specialist sports/health jobs involve degrees and postgraduate training such as working as sports physiotherapists, sport and exercise scientists, sports psychologists, sports injury specialists, sports nutritionists. Sports science degrees are a common way into this type of career, while some positions such as physiotherapists require specialist degrees. Often these careers may involve working with sports professionals at the peak of their careers, devising ways of helping them to achieve their full potential. Such careers require a long period of training and considerable academic study, but ultimately will lead to job opportunities with salaries from £18,000 to £50,000 a year.

CLUB AND CENTRE MANAGEMENT

With new centres being constantly opened, this is very much a growth area. Opportunities exist both in local councils and private businesses, including the increasing numbers of activity centres, spas and outdoor leisure activities such as paintballing. Management activities within health clubs and leisure centres are crucial to ensuring the success of a business. It is these people who are responsible for all the day-to-day tasks from administration, customer care, maintenance, ensuring everything is ready when an activity is due to start, to liaising with suppliers, customers and instructors. Experienced staff can find themselves involved in recruitment, training, arranging timetables, controlling budgets, special events and health and safety. Along the way there will also be opportunities to try out new sports, test facilities and expand your own sporting skills.

It is a job for people who like multi-tasking – who are capable of doing more than one thing at a time without panicking when things go wrong. There are many specialist roles which can be used as a means of entering management, such as being a lifeguard in a swimming baths. Starting as a marshal supervising games in a paintball company is a frequently used method of gaining experience before moving into site management. Depending on the location, you could be working outdoors for much of the time, or indoors undertaking tasks in a variety of settings. Shift work is common, as is working evenings, weekends and public holidays.

Long-term career prospects are good, either by remaining in management or moving into areas such as instructing or marketing. It could even provide a way of developing your own business in due course. Salaries start at around £12,000.

Sports development is a very specialised management activity. It is all about encouraging people to take part in events, using facilities that are already present, and developing new opportunities as they arise. It can involve a lot of meetings and administration, including dealing with budgets while working in a variety of locations. On the most basic level, sports development could involve looking at ways of getting a young offender involved in sport. At the other end of the spectrum, it could be investigating new sports and seeing if there is any market for them in the local area. It is unusual for people to enter such a specialised area without prior experience and training, particularly at degree level.

SPORTS MEDIA, MARKETING AND PR

Every day sport provides lots of news stories which have to be written for magazines and newspapers or broadcast on the TV, radio and websites. Events, personnel and key companies use the services of public relations and marketing specialists to drum up publicity and keep the public aware of what they are doing.

Some job opportunities within marketing and PR (public relations) are taken up by sports professionals coming to the end of their playing careers. But they tend to be in the minority and work mostly for themselves or larger organisations. Opportunities are to be had on local newspapers or in smaller companies. Most marketing, media and PR businesses are small and stick to a local area or work in one or just a few sports and activities. Sports photography is a specialist area. The vast range of organisations gives great scope for moving around the country, exploring new opportunities or working for yourself.

SPONSORSHIP AND SPORTS PROMOTION

Sponsorship is a growth area linking sports people with businesses. Agreements are made by which sportspeople are provided with money, products or services in return for allowing a company to use their name in advertising, helping with promotional work, raising awareness of the company within the community. People are needed to work within the industry organising and managing such deals.

Promoting sport is equally big business. Unless people know about activities they will not get involved, whether it is attending a football match, car race or marathon. Behind each event, there is an army of people intent on ensuring that the event goes smoothly and attracts a high audience. This involves marketing, PR and communication skills. It can involve long days, some travelling and lots of meetings. There are no set hours and weekend working is common, particularly if it involves attending sponsored events. Calls from the media can occur at any time of the day and even in the evenings in the run-up to a major activity.

Sports sponsorship, promotion and marketing have developed as specialist areas. Although some people may argue that they are no different from any other industry, specialist businesses have done a lot better than when general sponsorship and marketing organisations try to get involved in sport. As you are often promoting specific individuals or teams, a very detailed knowledge of the particular sport and the wider industry is vital. This is often an area that sport professionals move into when they can no longer compete at the highest level.

RETAILING

Specialist sports retailing is a growth area always seeking good staff. Helping people choose the best sports equipment requires skill, knowledge and sports expertise, which is why most sporting goods retailers employ keen sportspeople to sell their goods. Successful sports retailers are those that understand exactly what clothing and equipment is needed for a particular activity. Not everything is ready-made; equipment and clothing may have to be adapted or designed from scratch for a particular individual or activity.

ACTIVE LEISURE

The term 'active leisure' covers a wide range of roles such as holiday activity coordinators, play work and walking coordinators. It is a sector which is expanding fast, with new opportunities constantly emerging. Walking coordinators were unknown 10 years ago, yet are now found nationwide as councils seek to encourage people to go walking in parks and the countryside. Opportunities for holiday activity coordinators and play workers are extensive, both at home and overseas. Many travel companies and cruise ships employ people to work with children and young people, putting together programmes of events and organising them on a daily basis. Such work involves considerable flexibility and versatility – things often go wrong, instructors do not turn up and children have to be kept occupied. There is no average salary – it depends very much on the locality, the hours involved and the company. Sometimes it may be a full-time job, part time or just a few hours a week.

COMBINATION OF ROLES

While for larger organisations and businesses you may well be employed just in a specialist role, a huge majority of places of employment are much smaller and more local. So you will almost certainly have to combine a range of activities. For example, if you are an instructor, you may also have to do some management and office work, marketing, sales, maintenance and cleaning. A golf pro may spend much of their time instructing but will also be responsible for running a shop. If you are someone who likes to stick to a specific role, then this will certainly restrict your opportunities, both initially and during your career. Sport and active leisure is not an industry where you can get away with 'it's not my job to do that'.

PRACTICAL WORK

With sport and active leisure being a new and fast-growing sector, it is worth considering practical work, as it could offer a long-term career combined with discounted or free sport and activity benefits. Every building will need practical employees for maintenance of facilities, swimming pools, gardening, painting, secretarial and administrative roles, catering, car parking, security, and other roles that keep it all going.

You may start off at low-level practical work, and find you develop interests in particular sports or activities. While those without the relevant qualifications would not be considered by employers for specific roles as detailed in other types of work, organisations often have a policy of preferring internal candidates for available jobs. So if you show that in a practical work role you have been a good employee, you will stand a good chance of being considered for work you would not be offered if you approached as an external candidate.

Even if you have no plans to progress into other roles, practical work in this industry often means it is a more pleasant location and nicer atmosphere than doing the same job in an office, shop or factory. As a growing sector, it offers more job stability and opportunity too.

SELF-EMPLOYMENT OR RUNNING A BUSINESS

Increasing numbers of people are looking for self-employment opportunities or have long-term aims to have their own business. Sport and active leisure is ideal for this purpose. Instructors are frequently self-employed, and can build up a significant business over time. New business opportunities are constantly appearing which can appeal to those with an entrepreneurial bent. Just consider the number of unusual sports which have

---

BIRTH OF BUNGEE

Bungee jumping originated in Vanuatu, where islanders perform an annual ritual leaping 35 metres off a tower with vines tied to their ankles. The aim is to appease the gods and ensure a good harvest. Two New Zealanders recognised the potential of this unusual activity and adapted it using Latex rubber cords to establish the first commercial bungee jump. Variations on straightforward bungee jumping have emerged in New Zealand. How about bridge swinging – a gut-wrenching fall followed by a super-fast swing while harnessed to a cable? Then there is the bungee rocket, where you zoom upwards in a capsule, then bounce around like a yo-yo on a string!

---

taken root in the UK over the past decade – parakiting, zorbing, bungee jumping, paintballing and lasertag. In all of these cases, opportunities exist for entrepreneurs to develop a business, whether it is through provision of facilities, supplies or straight instruction. Robert McCracken, for example, started out as a marshal on a paintball site. He enjoyed it, became a manager on another site, and recognised there was a business opportunity. Linking up with some friends, he arranged finance and set up a branch of Skirmish in the Bristol area.

OVERSEAS TRAVEL

Sport and leisure is a global business requiring skilled staff. This means there are lots of opportunities for overseas travel. There are numerous employment possibilities, including lifeguards, recreation managers, fitness instructors, activity instructors, golf professionals, personal trainers, as well as management opportunities in sales/leisure and sports marketing. Cruise ships and international hotels frequently hire UK sport and leisure personnel.

UK qualifications and work experience are recognised throughout the world. However, some countries such as the USA may require people to pass additional federal qualifications. A good knowledge of foreign languages is recommended, especially if seeking work in Europe.

Obtaining a first aid qualification and keeping it updated is essential. Almost every job lists this as an essential skill. In addition, any sport and active leisure job which involves contact with or working with children will require you to undergo a CRB (Criminal Records Bureau) check. This is compulsory. Child protection training is also recommended. In addition, instructors will need professional indemnity insurance to provide cover in case something goes wrong while teaching. If someone is hurt while you are teaching them, there is a possibility they might sue you – and this can be costly.

APPRENTICESHIPS

Some jobs in this sector can be entered via an apprenticeship scheme. This allows people to train while working. Opportunities will depend on your area, as the range of apprenticeships available is linked into the local jobs market. For example, in London there are apprenticeship programmes in sport and leisure, activity leadership and sport, recreation teaching and instructing. There is also a link with Arsenal Football Club's community sports programme to offer a sport and leisure traineeship. To find out more about apprenticeships in your area, go to www.apprenticeships.org.uk.

CHAPTER 4
CASE STUDY 1

NICOLA TRIPPICK
Ice skater

Dedication has paid off for ice skater Nicola Trippick. Since turning professional in 2007, she has appeared on television shows, and participated in a major ice dance spectacular as well as developing a career teaching others.

Nicola began skating when she was 10.

'I just took to the ice very quickly and went to an Easter skating school where they told me I had some talent. I started having private lessons and just got better and better.

'I had a few partners and in 2003 won the Junior British Ice Dancing Championships. Then I went into the senior section with a new partner and eventually won a bronze medal in the Senior British Ice Dancing Championship.

'I enjoyed competing but eventually had to make some hard decisions and weigh up all the pros and cons. We had reached such a high standard that there were no coaches here that could work with us, so we were having to go to America to train. It meant that if I wanted to continue competing I would have had to move to America.

'Competing was very expensive. There was only a little sponsorship money available. You do not get paid for competitive skating. My parents helped me financially even after I left home. I worked at all kinds of part-time jobs to support my skating. I was a receptionist, sales executive, shop assistant and even worked as a waitress in a café.

'In 2007 I retired from competitive skating and turned professional. Since then I have taken part in ice shows. I got hold of the email address of the person responsible for hiring professional skaters for *Dancing on Ice Holland* and sent her my résumé. Several emails and phone conversations later I was offered a job as a skater partnering a celebrity. I flew out to Holland in October 2007 and stayed there for three months. My celebrity and I won the *Dancing on Ice* competition. The European tour of Holiday on Ice was in Holland at the time and we did several weeks of guest appearances.

'*Dancing on Ice* was the most amazing thing I have ever done so far. You had to really trust your celebrity, as they have to lift you up in the dance routines. I would definitely do it again.

'I have also trained as an ice-skating instructor and teach at Peterborough and Norwich. The training involved working with a mentor, lots of lectures and teaching practice. It takes nearly a year to do the Level 1 NISA Assistant Coach, which allows you to teach in group classes. I have gained Level 2, which allows you to be self-employed and work independently.

'I would like to do more shows and TV programmes and continue coaching. When opportunities come up I will take them.

'The younger someone starts skating, the better. You should never give up, no matter how hard it is – just keep at it. It is hard and you need a lot of dedication. There were times when my friends were going out and I had to go to bed because I was skating the next day – but, looking back, it was worth it.

'Even if you do not want to become a competitive skater there are opportunities available. If you are a good enough standard you can contact skating shows and agents or you can train as an ice-skating teacher. Teachers are always in demand; some clubs just do not have enough. Or you can work in an ice rink and get involved in the day-to-day operation of the rink.'

CHAPTER 5
TOOLS OF THE TRADE

Having decided that a career in sport and active leisure is for you, the big question that has to be answered is 'do you have the personal qualities that are needed to make a successful career?' Just enjoying doing sport and wanting to improve your sports abilities is not enough.

No matter what the job, everyone involved in the sport and active leisure industry shares certain key characteristics. An interest in one or more sports is obviously essential – you wouldn't want to spend the rest of your life doing something that bores you silly or that you really dislike!

You have to be prepared to work at your sports and develop your skills, trying new activities and broadening your qualifications. Although there will be opportunities to practise sports, remember that it will not always be at the level to which you are accustomed. If working as an instructor, you will often be spending your time teaching or coaching people new to a game or activity.

You must be willing to undertake your sport at a lower level than you are used to when teaching others.

FLEXIBILITY

A lot of flexibility is needed. This is not a career option for someone who likes a 9 to 5 routine existence. Working in sport and leisure means working shifts, weekends, evenings and public holidays. People come to use sports activities when they themselves have finished work – and that means that you have to be available when they need you. Some jobs may even be residential and expect you to be available overnight, particularly if it involves caring for horses. Travel within the UK or overseas may be required. All of this means that a career in sport and leisure can affect your personal life and relationships with friends. Your working hours may not match up with theirs – so you can have difficulty arranging times to meet up.

It is important to remember too that most careers in sport and leisure do not follow a clearly designated career path. You have to be willing to move from job to job to gain experience. In some cases this may mean moving around the country or even overseas. It is important to take advantage of opportunities as they arise.

DID YOU KNOW?

Although cricket is popular in many countries, only 10 are allowed to play in 5-day international games called test matches. These countries are India, Australia, Pakistan, Bangladesh, Sri Lanka, South Africa, New Zealand, Zimbabwe and England, as well as a group of Caribbean countries that play together as a team called the West Indies.

Seasonal work is extremely common within the industry. PGL is a major employer and provider of sporting activity holidays for children and young people in the UK and in Europe. It offers the majority of its positions on a fixed-term contract basis. This can be anything from 3 months to a full season of approximately 10 months. Other work has to be found when these periods of work are completed. Many activity instructors will often spend the spring/summer period in one location and then move on to a different site or company for the winter season. Around 50% of the fixed-term staff return to PGL each season. Once people become known to PGL and establish a reputation with them, longer-term contracts may become available for senior staff. Opportunities can also exist to join the permanent staff at head office or in centres.

COMMUNICATION SKILLS

Getting on with people from all walks of life is essential. You need to be able to talk to people, work with them and communicate easily. One day you might be dealing with groups of children, another day with the elderly or people with health problems or disabilities trying to get fit. Patience and a pleasant manner are essential.

You have to be good at dealing with people and communicating with them. It is important to be sociable, and able to work with all kinds of people. You need to be able to motivate them to improve their skills and encourage them to do better. Not everyone is good at sport and some may need a lot of encouragement and confidence-building.

To judge if you have these qualities, be honest and look at your own life. Being involved in activities such as Duke of Edinburgh's award schemes, youth work or sports coaching helps develop communication skills.

FIRST SURFERS

Most people would expect to find that surfing was invented by the Americans or Australians. In fact it wasn't. The real inventors could not be more different. Surfing is a water sport. It is done in the ocean or sea, where the surfer uses his or her surfboard to catch a wave, and ride in towards the shore. Surfing was invented by the Polynesians, at least 4,000 years ago. The Polynesians lived on a group of islands in the Pacific Ocean centred around the islands of Tonga, Samoa and Fiji.

TIMEKEEPING

Good timekeeping is essential, especially if you eventually aim to become a self-employed instructor. If you are constantly late for sessions, your clients will simply go elsewhere – leaving you with empty spaces on your timetable, which leaves less money coming in. Games and events tend to start on time, but you will often be needed some time before and after an event to arrange things and get equipment ready. Poor timekeeping has a knock-on effect, as it makes sessions and events after you late.

RESOURCEFULNESS

It is important not to panic easily. You need to have an ability to deal with problems as they arise, especially in emergencies. People may get hurt or upset, particularly in competitive games. You need to be able to deal with difficulties such as not enough or too many people turning up, locations being locked, transport breaking down, equipment being damaged or missing. If working with children as a play leader or in a holiday scheme, it is not unknown for instructors not to turn up – which could leave you suddenly in charge of 12 or more children looking for something to do.

First aid skills are not mandatory for every job, but for some activities and events organisations insist that there is at least one trained first aider, with a full kit, in charge. Obtaining first aid skills is useful for your career, but much more important than that is that, if something happens, you will know the basics of what to do or what not to do. It may even be you who is injured, and you will look a bit of an idiot if a member of the public asks you what needs to be done and you have no clue.

LEADERSHIP SKILLS

Enjoyment in doing the sport or activity itself is vital. If you are just doing it for the money and cannot wait to go home, your employers and paying customers will notice. Anyway, what better job is there than doing a sport or activity you like and getting paid for it?

An ability to deal with people of all ages and personalities is essential. Working in sport and leisure requires you to be good at motivating people and encouraging them when it is not going well. You have to be a good communicator and listener, to ensure your customers are getting what they want and need. You have to have the confidence to talk to people and an ability to address groups when necessary. You don't have to be an overpowering personality; just quietly confident enough to make it clear who is in charge. Possessing an ability to lead a group and having a lot of common sense are vital skills. Most people will be pleasant and a pleasure to deal with, but you will encounter aggressive, noisy, loud people who want everything their own way, and always know better than you how things should be done. You need enough forcefulness to tame these people and to know where to draw the line – such as with those who will not wear safety equipment or do things you have told them not to – yet without making the situation worse or by being too aggressive yourself.

PHYSICAL FITNESS

Most jobs require you to be physically fit, although there are examples of wheelchair-bound coaches, particularly when it comes to training disabled athletes, as well as disabled people working

BODYBOARDING

Riding the waves can be undertaken using bodyboards as well as surfboards. The difference relates to style and type of board. A bodyboard (often called a boogie board) is shorter and wider than a surfboard. It is made of pliable foam rather than fibreglass. Instead of standing up on a board as in surfboarding, the bodyboard rider lies flat and uses hands to steer, tilting the board when necessary. When you begin bodyboarding, you eat a tremendous lot of sand!

in support and administrative roles. Often the job will require you to move heavy equipment from one location to another. Remember, too, that if you are instructing or working in sports, and advocating a healthy lifestyle, you need to match what you are talking about. An unfit, overweight instructor will not inspire others. Actually, this is rarely a problem, as even if most of your work is at a desk, the ability to use the facilities for free encourages you to keep fit. In some jobs, the problem is not keeping fit, it is making sure you have almost as much energy left for a late-night session as you had for one before breakfast.

RESPONSIBILITY

You cannot take risks when working in sport and active leisure. It can result in danger to others, and increases the possibility of accidents. You have to be able to accept responsibility. You will need the confidence and authority to be prepared to recognise when there are problems and to stop people from behaving irresponsibly. If instructing, you will need to be willing to check out safety and take any precautions that are necessary. You need to be able to check equipment and places that are being used, and not be afraid to cancel or postpone a session or event if the equipment is faulty or there is a problem with lighting, or if someone has cleaned and polished the floor a bit too energetically.

EXPERIENCE

Experience is not always needed – as long as you have an enthusiasm for your sport and a willingness to learn – but it is unlikely that you will work in a sport or activity that you have never played or tried. Being energetic, dedicated and highly motivated will go a long way to overcome any lack of experience.

BUSINESS SKILLS

If aiming to be self-employed or run your own business, you will need basic business skills and awareness of tax and employment laws.

CHAPTER 6
FAQs

Q

What are the key considerations to bear in mind if opting for a job in this sector?

A

Working in sport and leisure does not mean you will simply play sports all day. You will have to be flexible about working hours, sociable and enjoy working with all kinds of people from those beginning a sport for the first time to those possessing a high level of expertise. You will need to be confident and provide the assistance required. You need to be confident dealing with people, able to accept responsibility and always aware of safety considerations.

Q

How do you know if it will suit you?

A

Having a keen interest in sport and active leisure is essential. If you can be flexible, willing to work hard and able to communicate easily with people, then this could be the career opportunity you have been looking for.

Weekends and evenings are the busiest times for sport and leisure locations. Many places take on staff purely for evenings and weekends. Even if you are unable to work full-time, you may be able to get casual work, particularly in the holidays. This will enable you to get a better idea of what the various jobs entail. Ask people who work there what they do, and how they got into it; most people are more than happy to talk about their work.

How much will I get paid?

Salaries vary from job to job. In general, expect a starting salary of around £10,000 depending on skills and qualifications. If food and accommodation are provided, this may be extra or taken into account in the final salary. Once trained, salaries can rise quite rapidly depending on the job you are doing, and how your career progresses. Play workers can earn up to £25,000 a year, while swimming pool technicians can earn £20,000+. A leisure centre assistant can earn anything between £14,000 and £18,000, sports development officers around £30,000, while full-time fitness trainers can earn up to £40,000.

DID YOU KNOW?

Physical education was first established in the 1944 Education Act, when its educational value was first recognised. Over the years, it has moved away from purely educational values towards physical recreation and, most recently, health-related fitness.

What are the working hours like?

There are no standard working hours. You will have to expect to be flexible over working hours. It is extremely rare for anyone to work office hours from 9 a.m. to 5 p.m., Monday to Friday. Shift work is common, as is working weekends and public holidays. You will have to expect to work when your friends are not working, and have time off when your friends are working.

How could my career progress?

The sky is positively the limit. There are no clear lines of progression. It is very much up to you as to where and how your career progresses. For example, an instructor could have a career which moves into human resources or personnel, into sports promotion or leisure centre management, into running a business or becoming self-employed, while someone working initially in leisure centre management may decide to move into administration, retail, play work or instructing. There will be lots

28 PERMANENT OLYMPIC GAMES

Only 28 sports are permanently included in the summer Olympic Games. Baseball and softball were dropped in 2005, leaving two spaces. Now the hunt is on for sports to fill the gap by 2016. Front runners are golf, karate, roller sport, rugby, squash – although baseball and softball are seeking a comeback. To become an Olympic sport, they have to prove that it is universally practised and has a high quality of competition. At stake is a need for the Olympics to engage with a new generation of sports fans, and fast – some sports have an ageing audience and fewer competitors. There are only five sports which have been contested at every summer Olympics since 1896: cycling, fencing, gymnastics, swimming, and track and field. Sports dropped from the Olympics over the years include duelling, stone-throwing, tug-of-war, rope climbing and lacrosse.

of opportunities to learn new skills, take up new sports and gain qualifications, and these can lead in many different directions.

Q **Where will I work?**

A Working locations depend entirely on the job. You may be working outside most of the time, or inside a leisure centre, shop, gym or swimming pool. You may be required to work at several different locations, travelling from place to place. What is certain is that you will not be sitting at a desk all day and every day.

Q **What are the opportunities for travel?**

A Sport and leisure is a global business requiring skilled people. UK qualifications are recognised throughout the world. Language skills will be needed if you are planning to work in continental Europe, but there are many other opportunities available on cruise ships, in activity holiday companies and within English-speaking countries. Holiday companies like PGL regularly recruit staff to work in centres worldwide, as do hotels and leisure companies.

How can I broaden my interest in sport or develop my own sports skills?

Start now by visiting your local leisure centre or water sports centre and finding out about new activities that are being offered. Try something unusual and see how you get on. Showing you are willing to explore and try out new activities, so as to broaden your experience, will impress potential employers.

When you are working in sport and leisure it becomes very easy to continue exploring new sports skills. There will be lots of opportunities to try out new sports, gain new qualifications and skills, as well as develop existing interests. It is up to you to take advantage of all the opportunities that are offered.

BIRTH OF BASEBALL

The all-American game of baseball actually has its origins in the UK, dating back to medieval times. There are medieval pictures showing participants playing a similar ball game with a bat. Then in 1744, a game called baseball is pictured in a publication of that year. The game is also mentioned in Jane Austen's *Northanger Abbey*. The UK version developed into rounders and this game was taken over to the US by settlers. This evolved into the game of baseball we know today. It was not until 1845 that Alexander Joy Cartwright Jr created the official rules of baseball and founded the first team – the Knickerbocker Base Ball Club.

CHAPTER 7
CASE STUDY 2

MARK LAVINGTON
Human Resources Manager PGL

Working in human resources was certainly not what Mark Lavington had in mind as a future career. His path to his present position has included teaching, canoe instructing, river leading, managing activity centres and training other staff.

His story begins when he learned to canoe whilst at university. He was offered holiday work by PGL as a canoeist in the Ardèche.

'I had a fantastic time, taking groups canoeing through a gorge. I met a lot of seasonal workers in the leisure industry whilst in the Ardèche and decided to take a year off. The result was several seasons working with PGL and I became a river leader. After a couple of years, I thought I had better try teaching, so obtained a job as a science teacher in Northamptonshire, where I ran the school canoe club. It was not very satisfying as I wanted to be out and about. In the summer, I was contacted by PGL and asked if I would manage a family centre based in Monmouth catering for 150 people with a staff of 25. I had a great time before going back to teaching but was already thinking of leaving. Then PGL contacted me and asked if I would run a windsurfing and sailing centre in the Mediterranean from Easter to September. I immediately resigned and went to PGL (much to my mum's discontent!).

'I thoroughly enjoyed my new life. The centre catered for 300 guests and had 120 staff. I spent the winter travelling, then came back to run PGL Mimosa. While running it I was talked into running a fledgling training department at PGL to investigate how to train staff. It was important to discover what the instructors wanted, and what types of qualifications were necessary. Eventually PGL offered me a permanent job in the training department. Over the next few years, the department grew from two people to 22, with a training programme that covers everything from full apprenticeships to NVQs and induction schemes.

'My role is now changing again, as I now have the responsibility of investigating new initiatives and projects which had previously been on the back-burner. This includes looking at opportunities for new business and training. My brief is simple – "go and find it and make it happen".

'I have never had a career programme. I have just been in the right place at the right time. I would never have imagined that this was the type of career I would have in the leisure industry, but I do not regret it. PGL has allowed me to enjoy my sports and develop an interesting career.

'I would recommend anyone interested in working in sport and leisure to be proactive and look for challenges. The opportunities are there.'

CHAPTER 8
TRAINING

There are many different ways of entering the sport and leisure industry. Many people enter it straight from school, via apprenticeships or after college or university courses. It can be entered at any age. Many skills such as administration and management are transferable, so skills learned in one job can be easily taken across to another. It doesn't matter what your background or skills are; there are job opportunities open to you.

From 2009, the Sport and Active Leisure Diploma (AQA/City & Guilds) will become a key qualification for 14- to 19-year-olds seeking to enter the industry. It aims to provide:

► an alternative to traditional learning styles
► work-related learning opportunities
► a relevant programme of learning to meet career requirements
► flexibility to progress straight into work or move into further or higher education
► essential skills and knowledge
► an opportunity to investigate different activities and industries within the sport and leisure sector
► a combination of theoretical study and practical learning.

Participants will mix classroom time with work at colleges and in local businesses. They will have to study English, maths and ICT, plus skills and subjects relevant to the sport and leisure industry. There will also be lots of hands-on experience.

PREMIER COSTS

A keen football fan will spend nearly £200,000 during their lifetime in supporting a club. Research carried out by Virgin Money indicated that supporters of Premiership clubs spend as much on their sport as they do on buying a home. Supporters pay around £1,875 each season, and taking inflation into account that comes to around £100,000 over a lifetime. Travel costs account for a further £40,000 in a lifetime, and another £25,700 being spent on club merchandise, food, drink and programmes.

This qualification will provide a good basis for developing a career in sport and leisure. It will give you the necessary background and basic skills for many of the jobs that are available. It will certainly give you a head start when it comes to interviews and seeking employment.

Another full time course is the BTEC First Diploma in Sport. There are two variations, one focusing on sport and the other concentrating on performance. Studied at college, this is equivalent to four GCSEs and aims to introduce people to the sport industry, giving a basis on which to progress to more advanced work-related qualifications. Depending on the diploma chosen, subject matter includes looking at health, safety and injury, the sports industry, planning and leading sports activities, nutrition, fitness and psychology for sports performance, lifestyle and the body in sport, as well as undertaking practical sport or outdoor and adventurous activities. Linked complementary subjects include Communication Studies Level 2, Numeracy Studies Level 2. Success in this can lead to other qualifications,

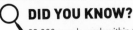

DID YOU KNOW?

88,000 people work within the British horse-racing industry in over 40 different jobs, covering everything from bookmakers to journalists, racecourse managers to trainers, jockeys to stable hands.

FIGURE 1
ACCESS TO: SPORT & ACTIVE LEISURE

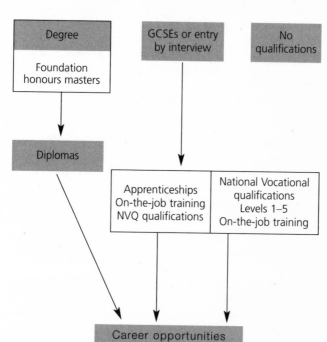

such as BTEC Higher Nationals in Sport and Leisure Management or Sport and Exercise Science, covering a range of work areas including fitness, coaching support and land/water-based outdoor pursuits. It can also prove to be a useful entry point into employment within leisure centres or sport-based jobs.

City & Guilds sport and leisure qualifications offer people a way of gaining a range of skills relevant to the industry. It ranges from Level 1 right up to Level 7, and covers both NVQ and vocational qualifications suitable to people starting out in the business, leading activities, supervising others or learning to manage a sports facility. Typical subject matter includes customer care, business knowledge, healthy lifestyles, outdoor adventure, exercise and fitness, swimming, playwork, safe working practices. Ultimately it can lead to a range of certificates and diplomas in a range of topics.

Employers require some GCSEs or some experience, evidence of interest in the sports industry, together with proof of good communication skills.

Sport and active leisure is a sector in which on-the-job training is common.

This form of training is possible for many careers within the sector, such as working in leisure centres or gaining instructors' qualifications. This involves studying for relevant NVQ qualifications and can be undertaken at college either full-time or on a day-release/part-time basis. Sometimes instructors qualified to train and assess candidates will train new entrants in a particular sport or activity within the working environment. This is very much hands-on learning.

If planning to do any form of teaching and instructing, you will need to obtain recognised qualifications. Each sport has its own national governing body and such qualifications can be obtained while working. For example, at PGL there are large-scale training programmes which help people obtain qualifications including apprenticeships, NVQs, National Governing Body coaching and personal competency awards. The range of skills that can be taught is enormous – PGL activity instructor Zoe Hartley has gained National Governing Body awards in quad biking, fencing and rifles, and has learned to lead archery, problem-solving sessions, orienteering and low ropes sessions; while Paul Harwood activity/surf instructor comments:

'Since joining PGL, I've gained my BSA Level 1 and Level 2 Surf Coach qualifications. I've even overcome my fear of heights to lead ropes activity sessions. I'd like to become a Surf Trainer/ Assessor in the future. As well as progressing with my surfing, I'd like to learn more about climbing and paddling, and increase my experience in outdoor activities.'

FIGURE 2
NATIONAL VOCATIONAL QUALIFICATIONS (NVQs)
SCOTTISH VOCATIONAL QUALIFICATIONS (SVQs)

These form work-based qualifications, which can be
obtained whilst doing a job.

Level 1
Foundation skills

Level 2
Semi-skilled tasks

Level 3
Craft, skilled and supervisory tasks

Level 4
Technical, junior management skills

Level 5
Specialist skills leading to professional status
and senior management positions

First aid qualifications are often required. Training may be
provided by employers but it can also be obtained by contacting
organisations such as the St John Ambulance and Red Cross. It is
recommended that anyone involved in instructing or working with
children should have this qualification.

Sport and active leisure can be a risky business. Accidents can
happen – with serious or even fatal consequences. This is why
training is so essential.

In 1993, four teenagers were drowned at Lyme Bay during a
kayaking exercise. The subsequent trial led to the prosecution of
the centre manager and the company owning the outdoor activities
site, resulting in a conviction for corporate manslaughter.

Following the Lyme Bay disaster, licensing was introduced for a range of activities in 1996. It has become a legal requirement under the Activity Centres (Young Person's Safety) Act 1995 for providers of certain types of activity to undergo inspections of safety systems and acquire a licence. The Adventure Activities Licensing Service – an independent inspection body run by the Health and Safety Executive – is responsible for these inspections. Licensable activities include rock climbing, abseiling, ice climbing, gorge walking, sea-level traversing, canoeing, kayaking, dragon boating, wave skiing, white water rafting, improvised rafting, sailing, sailboarding, windsurfing, hill walking, mountaineering, fell running, orienteering, pony trekking, off-road cycling, off-piste skiing, caving, potholing and mine exploration.

DID YOU KNOW?

Football is football – or is it? There are numerous variations such as American football, Gaelic football, Australian rules football and Canadian football. And, despite being played with a different-shaped ball, rugby is actually regarded as a version of football: rugby league football and rugby union football.

Degrees are essential for careers such as sports development, sports science or sports therapy. There are also degree opportunities in areas such as sports marketing. This will require a minimum of three years' study at university. Be very sure this is what you want before starting out. There is a lot of competition for jobs in these sectors and there is no guarantee of a job. Getting a degree is expensive. A first degree now costs at least £12,000 and this figure is not going to decrease; on top of this, you have to pay living expenses. Loans are available but these do have to be paid off in instalments once you start work.

If you are not sure about your course or career choice, then there is much to be said for exploring other options. You can still opt for a degree course later in your career. It is a big commitment in time and money.

CHAPTER 9
CASE STUDY 3

MARK DUNGAR
Lifeguard

Swimming as a hobby has led to an interesting career opportunity for teenager Mark Dungar.

'I was due to go into the sixth form, but dropped out as it was not right for me. I had been a member of Diss Otters Swimming Club for many years and had trained as a lifeguard. This had enabled me to work as a casual lifeguard at Diss swimming pool. When I dropped out of sixth form, the management at Diss swimming pool offered me a full-time job as a lifeguard.

'I have been working here for a year. Apart from acting as a lifeguard within the pool, I help keep it clean and do back washes – filling up the chlorine barrels and making sure they do not get empty.

'I enjoy my job. It is not what I had expected. I thought I would be sitting all day just watching the pool. It is much more than that. There are lots of opportunities to expand my skills. I am working with different age groups in a very friendly environment. I meet a lot of people every day; you get to know people who come regularly. I get one month's holiday every year, which can be taken whenever I want.

'The biggest drawback has been the hours. There are different shift patterns: one day you can be on early, another on late. It makes my social life very difficult but I can accept that because I can see my career developing.

'My skills have expanded. I have done a health and safety course focusing on how to do risk assessments and also a gym instructor's course. A gym instructor here at the centre suggested I would be good at it. I wanted to widen my career paths and thought it would be a good idea. I have passed my practical and am waiting for the results of my theory exam. Once I have this qualification, I will continue doing some lifeguarding and also work as a gym instructor. I will continue getting more qualifications.

'I have an appraisal meeting with my line manager every six months and we look at what qualifications I could get, how my career can develop. I would like to continue working here, get as many qualifications as I can, including that of swimming teacher, and eventually become a deputy manager in charge of the centre.

'I have no regrets about not going into the sixth form. It was not for me. I learn more from hands-on work rather than sitting behind a desk. This is providing me with an interesting and challenging career, which I had not expected, yet doing things I enjoy. I would recommend it to anyone.'

CHAPTER 10
THE LAST WORD

Having read this book, you should now have a good idea as to whether a career in sport and active leisure offers you the opportunities you are looking for.

For the right person, this is a sector which can offer tremendous job satisfaction and career development. You will certainly not be bored! Some people may still be uncertain. This does not mean that the sector is wrong for you; it just means you need more time to think. This book does not set out to be comprehensive, answering every question you might possibly have about the sector. Instead it aims to give an overview and guidance on what it means to work in sport and active leisure. There is much more that can be learned.

Anyone who is seriously considering a sport and active leisure career should try to obtain some work experience doing the type of jobs you are interested in. It is the only way in which you can really find out what the work entails and whether you would like it or not. It also looks good on your CV and may lead to work opportunities. Talk to people who are already working in the industry; find out about their jobs and career development. Ask them for advice – they will be only too willing to help. Contact companies working in the type of sport in which you are interested and ask about career opportunities.

If you are already in work and looking for a career change, getting work experience is still essential. Use holiday leave or work at

BIRTH OF BASKETBALL

Basketball was invented in 1891 by a Canadian PE teacher called Dr James A. Naismith in Massachusetts. The state is renowned for its cold winters and Naismith wanted a sport that could be played indoors during the winter. The initial goals were peach baskets, and players had to climb a ladder to remove the ball after scoring a goal. Then some bright spark (no one knows who) hit on the idea of removing the bottom of the basket. Soon afterwards the peach baskets were replaced by simple metal rings with netting.

weekends and public holidays – remember that the sport and active leisure sector is busy 365 days a year. Regard it as an investment in your future.

After undertaking some work experience, if you still believe this is the career for you the next step has to be looking at entry options and obtaining any qualifications that are necessary.

Ask yourself:

▶ Do you have the right qualifications to begin a career in sport and leisure?

▶ Do you need any further training?

▶ Can you get on-the-job training or do you need to attend a college course?

▶ How can you convince potential employers of your keenness?

Use the Further Information section which follows to find answers to these and other questions you may have. There are lots of organisations waiting to help you develop your qualifications and career prospects within an expanding industry.

Finally, have a look through this checklist to see if you have the skills required to make a career in sport and active leisure.

Tick Yes or No

Are you a good timekeeper?	☐ Yes	☐ No
Are you good at sports?	☐ Yes	☐ No
Are you willing to try new sports?	☐ Yes	☐ No
Are you good with people?	☐ Yes	☐ No
Can you think on your feet and come up solutions in a hurry?	☐ Yes	☐ No
Can you teach others?	☐ Yes	☐ No
Are you calm, patient, reliable, responsible?	☐ Yes	☐ No
Do you like variety?	☐ Yes	☐ No
How flexible are you?	☐ Yes	☐ No
Do you mind working weekends, evenings or bank holidays?	☐ Yes	☐ No

If the answers are mainly 'Yes' in each case, then a career in sport and active leisure may be right for you. The hard part then is to decide just which of the many career options is the one you want.

CHAPTER 11
FURTHER
INFORMATION

Listed in this section are contact details for organisations that can provide information and advice about careers and qualifications within the sport and active leisure sector.

GENERAL INFORMATION

SkillsActive

Castlewood House,
77–91 New Oxford Street,
London WC1A 1PX
Tel 020 7632 2000
www.skillsactive.com

This is the sector skills council for the active leisure and learning industry. It monitors and aims to improve the supply of skills training.

Edexcel

Tel 0870 240 9800
www.edexcel.com

Edexcel is the UK's largest awarding body for academic and vocational qualifications. There is a Subject Advisors Service, which can offer advice on qualifications in PE and BTEC Sport. They can be contacted on 0844 576 0036 or via email at PEandSportSubjectAdvisor@edexcelexperts.co.uk

AQA/City & Guilds Diploma

www.diplomainfo.org.uk/AQA-city-and-guilds-diplomas.asp

Connexions

www.connexions.gov.uk
www.connexions-direct.com/jobs4U

These sites provide careers information for young people and have links to local Connexions offices. You can also find detailed job descriptions and profiles of people working in different areas of sport and leisure, helping you to get a feel for what a job is like.

Careers Advice

www.careersadvice.direct.gov.uk/helpwithyourcareer/jobprofiles/category29

A very useful website containing lots of information about careers, job profiles and advice on applying for jobs. Category 29 is the category for sport and leisure.

Institute of Sport, Parks and Leisure (ISPAL)

Tel 0118 929 8356
www.ispal.org.uk

This is a trade organisation dealing with the sport and leisure sector. It offers lots of career information, lists of specialist recruitment agencies and relevant organisations.

Sports Industries Federation (SIF)

www.sportsdata.co.uk

This is a UK federation of 28 associations and groups involved in sports retailing, manufacturing and management. It provides links to member associations as well as news and information.

Become instantly more attractive

To employers and further education providers
Whether you want to be an architect (Construction and the Built Environment Diploma); a graphic designer (Creative and Media Diploma); an automotive engineer (Engineering Diploma); or a games programmer (IT Diploma), we've got a Diploma to suit you. By taking our Diplomas you'll develop essential skills and gain insight into a number of industries. Visit our website to see the 17 different Diplomas that will be available to you.
www.diplomainfo.org.uk

INFORMATION ON SPECIFIC JOB AREAS

Fitness Industry Association

Tel 020 7420 8560

www.fia.org.uk

National Register of Personal Trainers (NRPT)

Tel 0870 200 6010

www.nrpt.co.uk

National Association of Karate and Martial Arts Schools (NAKMAS)

Tel 01227 370055

www.nakmas.co.uk

Swimming Teachers' Association (STA)

Tel 01922 645097

www.sta.co.uk

British Horse Society (BHS)

Tel 0844 848 1666

www.bhs.org.uk

Association of British Riding Schools (ABRS)

www.abrs-info.org

Professional Golfers' Association

Tel 01675 470333

www.PGA.info

Lifesavers: The Royal Lifesaving Society UK (RLSS)

Tel 01789 773994

www.lifesavers.org.uk

British Racing School

www.brs.org.uk